JEFFREY WALLACE, MIKE HAMMER, & MATTY MCCAGE

99 THINGS

EVERY
GUY
SHOULD
KNOW

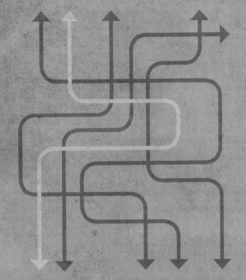

NAVIGATING RELATIONSHIPS, SUCCESS,
AND LIFE'S OTHER BIG STUFF

YouthMinistry.com/TOGETHER

99 Things Every Guy Should Know
Navigating Relationships, Success, and Life's Other Big Stuff

© 2013 Jeffrey Wallace, Mike Hammer, & Matty McCage

group.com
simplyyouthministry.com

Credits
Authors: Jeffrey Wallace, Mike Hammer, & Matty McCage
Executive Developer: Nadim Najm
Chief Creative Officer: Joani Schultz
Editor: Rob Cunningham
Cover Art and Production: Veronica Preston

Unless otherwise noted, all Scripture quotations are taken from the *Holy Bible*, New Living Translation, copyright © 1996, 2004, 2007 by Tyndale House Foundation. Used by permission of Tyndale House Publishers, Inc., Carol Stream, Illinois 60188. All rights reserved.

Scriture quotations marked NIV are taken from THE HOLY BIBLE, NEW INTERNATIONAL VERSION®, NIV® Copyright © 1973, 1978, 1984, 2011 by Biblica, Inc.™ Used by permission. All rights reserved worldwide.

ISBN 978-0-7644-9136-8

10 9 8 7 6 5 4 3   20 19 18 17 16 15 14 13

Printed in the United States of America.

TABLE OF CONTENTS

INTRODUCTION

Writing this book brought back so many memories of life as a teenager. Pimples, crazy hairstyles, reversible sweatshirts, overhaul shorts—those were some good times! The three of us grew up in a different era from you, and every now and then, our friends and family members pull out awkward photos and tell embarrassing stories from those days. (Don't laugh too hard—this will happen to you someday, too!) And though the context of our teenage years differs from yours, we still struggled with the same issues of life as you do. It's part of being a guy!

We really hope you enjoy the book, laugh at our stupidity, and take some of it to heart. Don't treat it like a textbook. Feel free to bounce around and focus on the areas that are most important to you right now. Sometimes you'll see that one of us is sharing a personal story; other times we've put our brains together to offer some collective wisdom and advice.

But before we cut you loose, there's one ultimate thought we want you to walk away with.

No matter where you are in your spiritual journey, there is a Creator who desires more than anything to be your Father. We understand that not everyone who reads this book has a great father/son relationship. Some of you can't wait to see your dad today, some are dreading when he'll walk through the door, and others of you have never met your dad. Regardless of your situation, please know that God's greatest longing for you is to move from being his *creation* to being his *child*. In God's arms you'll find love, encouragement, wisdom, healing, and life. That's the greatest and most basic thought you ought to know.

Know that you're loved and prayed for!

Jeffrey, Mike, and Matty

CHAPTER 1

RELATIONSHIPS

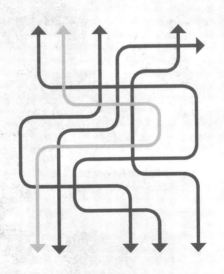

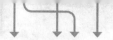

3 THOUGHTS ABOUT FAMILY

1. MAINTAIN REALISTIC EXPECTATIONS

I (Matty) was raised by imperfect parents. There were times I felt they grew angry too quickly, yelled too loudly, and punished too harshly. While we can debate whether my memories of those situations are accurate or not, a couple of things are certain: *I pushed my parents to the limit, and they loved me more than I'll ever know.*

One day my children will tell their friends how I snapped to conclusions, yelled to the point where I went hoarse, and threatened to throw away every toy they owned. They will recall how imperfect I was (and am). But one thing they will know for sure is that I loved them more than I could fully show them.

Parenting isn't easy, and parents make mistakes. Trust me when I say, "We know when we blow it, and we're not happy about it either."

2. FAMILY IS WHAT YOU MAKE OF IT

Last night, my wife, Joyce, and I (Matty) watched our kids eat dinner at the table. They were full of smiles, laughter, and happiness. I was amazed at how much they not only loved each other but also loved to be together. I asked Joyce if she had similar memories from her childhood, and she did.

I don't have many memories of my sisters and me getting along that well. It's not that we didn't love each other; we just didn't know how to get along. Families aren't void of conflict but overcome conflict together. Families aren't fully put together but require a lot of assembly (you'll hate that term when you become a dad).

Your family is just that: *your family.* It is what you make of it. Take ownership and choose to make great memories full of love and excitement.

3. FAMILY LOVE IS A VAGUE LOVE

Every person has a way they feel love. Some people respond well when someone says something nice and nurturing to them, and others respond better if something is done for them. In his book *The Five Love Languages*, author Gary Chapman identifies five "languages" or ways of communicating love: *words of affirmation, physical touch, receiving gifts, quality time, and acts of service.*

Before concluding that your family doesn't love you, first decide which language you respond to best. Then write down each one of your immediate family members and their love language next to their name. Chances are they're showing they love you in the same method they respond to best.

Remember, love can be a very confusing thing for people to show. Most parents simply reflect the way they were raised and were shown love. Love not only requires us to have an open heart but an open mind as well.

3 THOUGHTS ABOUT FRIENDS

4. LEARN TO PRACTICE DISCERNMENT

Not everyone needs to be in your space. To be honest, not everyone has earned that right. My grandmother (Matty here) used to always remind me as I was getting older, "You're known by the company you keep." At first I thought she was crazy, but then I noticed the look in her eye and realized she wasn't crazy—she was dead serious!

I made a lot of bad decisions (and a few *really* bad ones) as I was growing up, and none of them were made on my own. Someone was always there convincing me to make a bad choice, or I was willing to compromise everything for another person. Either way, if I had surrounded myself with better people, I would probably have fewer "scars" and less "baggage" to deal with today.

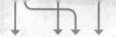

5. IT'S ALL ABOUT YOUR VERTICAL

Growing up, playing basketball was one of my (Matty here) favorite things to do. I would spend every chance I could on the driveway dribbling my "Dr. J" basketball and imagining I was Isaiah Thomas running a fast break for the Pistons. Every time, when I would drive the lane, I would stretch myself a little more in the hopes of slamming the ball down with all fury and ripping the rim off the backboard. But I had one HUGE problem: My vertical was weak!

I tried every day to jump a little higher than before, and as my vertical grew so did my confidence. When we think about our relationships, everything really hinges on how healthy our "vertical" is. Where is your relationship with God right now? If you're not sure, look at your friendships. As our relationship with God grows stronger (our vertical), we will have healthier friendships and will choose them more wisely. And as our relationship with God grows, so will our confidence.

6. KNOWING WHEN TO LET A "FRIEND" GO

I (Matty) am an emotional hoarder. I hate letting relationships go and will hold on to them until the bitter end—and even then I have a hard time letting go. There are people on my contact list that haven't responded to text messages from a year ago, yet I can't let go. What if they come back around? What if they decide to accept my apology? What if they change?

To be honest, I need to "let go" of a lot of people. The relationships weren't healthy (*unhealthy* doesn't always mean *unholy*), and would do well to move forward. A good rule of thumb I have to remind myself to live by is, *"If I feel the need to 'please,' then I need to say 'peace.'"*

3 THOUGHTS ABOUT ENEMIES

7. YOU'VE GOTTA LET IT GO

One of the biggest struggles in my life (Matty) has been letting go of the anger and hurt I feel when someone lies to me, hurts me, or betrays me. My first (and most honest) reaction is to either verbally unload on them or let my fist have a conversation with their face. Basically, I want to hurt them back. Unfortunately, while that might help me feel vindicated, neither of these approaches gets me anywhere.

I think this is why Jesus said to "turn the other cheek." At first I thought this was a weak approach and that Jesus was wussing out. As I've gotten older, I've realized Jesus wants me to turn the other cheek so I can have a heart that honors him and works to forgive those who mess with me. It wasn't a weak approach he was teaching, but a meek one.

8. PEOPLE ARE GOING TO HURT YOU

Getting hurt really bites! No one wakes up in the morning hoping someone is going to trash their reputation, post something hurtful on a social media site, or stab them in the back. Yet somehow it feels like we have a neon target on our backs, begging for someone to blast us.

The reality is that everyone has someone in their life who's hurt them, and we can't control that. What we can control is if we choose to respond with forgiveness when that person hurts us or if we react with emotion and, in turn, hurt someone else.

9. LEARN TO RESPOND AND NOT REACT

One of my "claims to fame" (Matty here) as a teenager was how quickly I could lose my temper. I could go from 0 to 60 in 2.2 seconds if someone pushed the right button—and when that happened, look out! I was the king of reacting to situations with emotion and anger.

If you hit me, I was going to hit you harder. If you said something to me, I was going to yell louder or be more sarcastic. No matter what, I was going to top whatever you did to me.

The result: I hurt the wrong people (those who actually cared about me), I hurt too many people (just about everyone I knew), and people stopped hanging out with me (I ended up being a loner). The reality: I had to learn to respond, not react. Whether it was my parents putting me in the middle of their divorce, my teachers disrespecting me in front of my friends, or a girl cheating on me, I had to learn to take a moment, calm down, and respond to the situation with logic and common sense.

5 THOUGHTS ABOUT AUTHORITY

10. EVERYONE HAS TO SUBMIT TO SOME KIND OF AUTHORITY

We like to make decisions. We were created with free will, which means we were created to make decisions. If we're honest, sometimes we wish we could just do whatever we wanted to do and not have to worry about the consequences. But we know it's not that easy because every choice has consequences. We will have to answer to someone in authority.

Regardless of your position or status in life, you will have someone in authority over you. It may be a parent, a teacher, law enforcement, a boss, or some other authority figure. Even the president has people that he (or she) must answer to and rules that have to be followed. Ultimately, we are all under the authority of God.

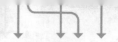

You may not like it, but we all have someone in authority over us. Our responsibility is to respectfully submit to authority. The sooner we accept that, the better we can understand how to live our best life.

11. OBEDIENCE DOESN'T ALWAYS EQUAL HONOR AND RESPECT

I (Matty) hated cleaning my dog's poop from our back door. For some reason my mom decided to train Taffy to do her business right in the doorway where our unexpected guests would be greeted with a fresh surprise whenever they walked into the house. While this never made sense to me, the fact that I as the boy of the family had to clean it up multiple times a day made even less sense.

It never failed that as I was getting ready to beat a level on Atari® (look it up online), Taffy would decide to take care of business. Without fail I would have to stop what I was doing (which I didn't want to do) to take care of the present she left me (which I *really* didn't want to do).

One day as I threw my controller down (reacted) and stomped through the kitchen, my mom (7 inches shorter than me) stopped me in my tracks with these words: "Matthew Dale, you better get your attitude in check!"

Completing my chore (family pooper scooper) wasn't what my mom was teaching me. The real lesson was this: The greatest sign of respect is not just following the instruction, but following it with the right attitude.

12. YOUR CIRCUMSTANCE DOESN'T DETERMINE YOUR RESPONSIBILITY

We cannot always choose every circumstance of life. We will be in situations that we just don't like. That can include not liking or agreeing with someone who is in authority over us. *So anyone who rebels against authority is rebelling against what God has instituted (Romans 13:2)*. That does not mean people in authority will always make the right choices every time. But it does mean God designed us to operate with a system of authority. It exists for our benefit.

Whether or not you share the same perspective with those in authority does not change your responsibility to respect authority. Sharing your thoughts in a respectful way can be acceptable, but ultimately God calls you to obey.

13. TRUE AUTHORITY DOESN'T AIM TO HURT

Authority exists for our benefit. That's the simple goal. True authority is not selfish. Actually, the whole reason for authority should be to create the best situation possible for everyone involved. Even when a person in authority uses corrective measures or enforces consequences, the ultimate goal still should be an outcome of good.

We also know that not everyone is perfect. People make wrong choices (that includes all of us). At times, people in authority step over the line and abuse their position by mistreating someone they are in authority over. That is not OK. Sometimes the best way we can respect authority is to hold people accountable when they have abused their positions.

If you have ever been in a situation where someone has abused you, what that person did is not acceptable. Respecting authority does not mean keeping quiet about what happened. Remember that they, too, have to operate under authority. Tell someone else in a role of authority. Make it known.

14. SEEK OUT AN AUTHORITY FIGURE TO SPEAK INTO YOUR LIFE

It's been said that there are two ways to learn something: (1) You can learn it the hard way, or (2) you can learn it from someone who learned it the hard way. The three of us can't speak for you, but we would rather learn a lot of things without having the bad experiences and pain! Learning from others helps us to avoid the same mistakes and shows us the best choices to make.

Your challenge is to be intentional about finding an authority figure—aka, a mentor. Find someone who lives in a way that you want to be like him.

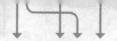

Maybe it's your father, an uncle, a teacher, a youth worker, or a man at your church. Whoever it is, find someone that you can go to with questions, and learn from him. You will be that much better off and can make decisions that will take your life in a better direction.

CHAPTER 2

FINANCES

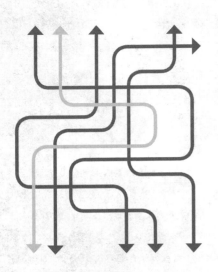

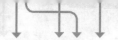

3 THOUGHTS ON STEWARDSHIP

15. IT'S NOT YOURS TO BEGIN WITH

When I (Matty) was growing up, I had a gerbil named Georgie. For the life of me, I still can't recall why I gave the overgrown rat such an odd name, but for some reason I did. I also don't remember how I ever convinced my parents to buy Georgie in the first place! But I remember thinking he was the coolest thing—until he died.

Georgie was fun, but he was delicate. When I picked him up, I had to be careful with him. I had to hold him tight enough so he didn't fall out of my hands (and run through the house) but not too tight to where he would pee on me. Similarly, money requires a gentle balance of holding on just tight enough to use it correctly but not too tight to where it becomes all about us.

If we forget that our financial blessings come from God in the first place, we'll lose all perspective and end up with nothing in the end.

16. BE INTENTIONAL WITH YOUR PERSPECTIVE

Perspective means everything. A wrong perspective can convince you that having lots of money makes you better than someone else. And a wrong perspective can convince you that what you don't have makes you second-rate. Regardless of what you have or don't have, never lose sight of the fact that money is a tool that God gives us to take care of business and to build his kingdom.

17. APPRECIATE WHAT YOU HAVE, AND EXERCISE WISDOM

I (Matty) love my boys. I mean, I love them a ton. Because I love them, I love to buy them good things.

And because of that, it gets super frustrating to head out the door, expecting them to have their iPods® in hand, only to see them empty-handed. It never fails: When I ask them where their iPods are, they stare at me like I'm speaking Klingon!

As we get older, we tend to want the "latest and greatest." While there isn't anything wrong with wanting something, we have to take care of what God's blessed us with and with what has been provided to us. I need to take care of what I have and help make it last as long as I can. It's the crazy concept called "stewardship."

3 THOUGHTS ON SAVINGS & INVESTMENT

18. DO A LOT WITH LESS

Jesus taught a parable in the Bible about a man who was heading out on a trip and who entrusted three servants with varying amounts of money to manage while he was gone. Each servant formulated a game plan and executed it to perfection while the boss was gone. When he returned, they were excited and full of anticipation as they expected to be congratulated for a job well done. But what one of them received was the total opposite.

One had buried his money in the ground, while the other two found a way to legally double their money. Upon seeing this, the boss was ecstatic for the two who invested wisely but was angry with the guy who buried his money. (You can read the whole thing in Matthew 25:14-30.) Here is the lesson: You can't always control how much money you get, but you can control what you do with it.

19. DON'T BLOW IT

My (Matty here) first "real" job as a teenager was at a local fish joint, and man, did it stink. Literally! When my sister picked me up from work, she made me hold my work shirt out the window!

My job responsibilities ranged anywhere from taking out the garbage to cleaning the shipment of fish when it arrived. Do you know what I was paid for this awesome job? A whopping $3.80 an hour! (Yes, minimum wage was $3.80 an hour back in the day.)

Fridays were a mixture of emotion because it was our busiest day of the week but was also payday. While my checks weren't huge, my dad taught me this principle: "Son, give God 10 percent, give yourself 10 percent, and the rest—put in the bank." At first the amounts seemed so small—until I bought my first two cars with my own cash.

20. MAKE FOR TODAY, AND SAVE FOR TOMORROW

When I (Matty) turned 18, my dad decided I was ready for "the talk." We sat at our favorite restaurant on a Saturday morning ready to order our "usual." And that's when he dropped the bomb. You could tell he was a little nervous, but he had thought this through. I squirmed a little in my chair because I didn't think I was ready for this conversation. And then my dad, full of passion and planning, addressed the elephant in the room.

"Son, you're getting older, and soon you're gonna get married. Here's something you need to know." (Oh great.) "Before you know it, you'll be ready to retire, and you need to be prepared." "What?!? Retired? " "Yes, son. You need to start saving now. The difference in waiting a decade can be a million bucks." Ever since then, my dad has asked me the uncomfortable questions to hold me accountable. Now I'm 35 and married with three children, and I have to admit that my dad was right. Time (and money) will fly before your eyes. You never have as much time as you think.

3 THOUGHTS ON GIVING

21. THE MORE YOU GIVE, THE MORE YOU RECEIVE

Have you ever been in a situation where you've done a kind gesture for someone else, and it made you feel good? Maybe you've helped a neighbor, or served in a soup kitchen, or spent time with someone who needed a friend. Those can be some of the most rewarding moments in life. People who give are often the happiest people you will ever know.

We get to make a lot of choices about our time, our talents, and our resources, including money. When you use any of those for the benefit of others, God honors that. When you give from what you have, you not only help someone else, but you also get to experience reward in different forms. It may be a sense of satisfaction. It may be greater opportunities. It may be some sort of financial blessing.

We do not have all that we have just to keep for ourselves. Share what you have for the benefit of others, and you'll reap the results of your generosity.

22. THE MORE YOU RECEIVE, THE MORE YOU CAN GIVE

Take a moment and think about every good thing you have ever received. If you're reading this, then you've been on the receiving end of sight, light, oxygen, a functioning body, and life—just to name a few. Sometimes we take things for granted. Let's be honest: We like to get things. The danger is that we can get so caught up in receiving that we miss out on the gift of giving. Giving is our opportunity to add benefit to someone else's life. God does some incredible things with this, so pay attention: When you receive something, you are blessed. You are being provided for. Then, when you have something to give, you get to bless someone else PLUS you get to receive the benefit of knowing you've helped.

The less we hold on to what we have and the more we use it for the benefit of others, the more God will bless us in ways we cannot imagine. Be less about holding on and more about giving, and your life will be better for it.

23. GIVING IS AN ACT OF WORSHIP

When you give something, it can seem to go against what we sense inside our mind. We can have this attitude that we should watch out for ourselves. *Take care of me. Make sure I have what I want.* What if we stopped thinking of everything we have as stuff that belongs to us, and instead looked at it as something that belongs to God but is given to us to use while we're here? That's called stewardship. This changes everything.

Maybe you've worked to earn money for a car or a computer or phone. At the end of the day, those things will not matter. What matters is what you do with what you have. Are they just for you? Or are you using them to make a difference in the world? We don't *have* to give.

We *get* to give. It's an opportunity for us to say, "God, everything is yours. Everything I have is yours. I only have it because you've allowed it, and I believe you will continue to provide. Help me to use what I have in ways that honor you." With this perspective, you'll never look at what you have the same way again.

4 THOUGHTS ON FINANCIAL BASICS

24. OUTGOING CAN'T EXCEED YOUR INTAKE

The reality is, you're only going to make so much money in your lifetime. No matter how many degrees you earn, connections you make, or skills you develop, it seems as if there is a natural cap on what most people make, which you really can't control. So work as hard as you can and make what you can. But while you can't always determine how much you make, you can control how much you spend.

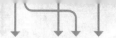

The most basic but essential rule of thumb is to make sure what you spend every month doesn't exceed what you bring home. In fact, if you want to be really wise, spend a lot less than your income (it helps this crazy thing called savings). This is a good habit to learn now, before your financial math equation has a whole lot of zeros added to it.

25. KEEP YOUR DEBT DOWN

As you get older, your taste for things increases. Soon, you'll transition from gaming systems to cars, and from Hot Pockets® to bachelor pads. By the time you graduate from college, it's possible that you may owe more than $50,000 in college loans. The crazy thought is that having debt seems pretty much unavoidable for most people.

Danger comes into play when we convince ourselves that a new pair of shoes or dinner for a date is something worth charging on a credit card.

If we're not careful, a suffocating amount of debt can sneak up on us and financially take us out. And while this is true, just remember that debt that might be considered "good" or "acceptable" is something that directly benefits your life and makes you more money in the end.

26. DON'T LET FINANCES CONTROL YOU

Regardless of whether you agree or disagree with the majority of this section, please wrap your arms around this thought: Please don't let your finances control your life. Yes, you will have to make money and you will incur expenses. But you don't want to be obsessed with this whole process. A lot will be out of your control, but you can always make it worse or better with your decisions.

Common sense will be your greatest ally. Don't ignore it. It doesn't matter how great of a deal you might find; if you can't afford it, you can't afford it. If you can't afford something, walk away.

27. KNOW THE DIFFERENCE BETWEEN A WANT AND A NEED

I (Matty) am a super impatient person. I know what I want, and when I want something I figure out how to make it happen. What got me in the most financial trouble was when I found something cool but didn't patiently decide if the thing was a "need" or a "want." Pretty soon, every "want" became a "need," and before I knew it I got behind on what adults like to call "financial obligations" (bills). By the time I started to get a handle on things, too much had gotten out of control. Use this time in your life to start a great financial habit of learning to tell yourself no. Your middle-aged self will thank you.

CHAPTER 3

DATING & SEX

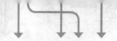

Sadly in life, when it comes to love, sex, and relationships, culture upholds a great double standard between girls and guys. If a girl is in a lot of relationships or has sex with a lot of people, she is labeled with a derogatory name, but if a guy has sex with a lot of girls, he is crowned king and is viewed as "the man." That's the way the world sees it. But when the Bible teaches us to flee sexual immorality (1 Corinthians 6:18-20) or not to conform to the ways of this world (Romans 12:1-2), God is talking to both girls and guys.

When it comes to sex and dating, as a young man it's your responsibility to always be a gentleman. Sex is an amazing thing that God blessed and ordered for marriage. If a girl is worth your time, she's worth you respecting her body. She is someone's daughter, granddaughter, niece, and sister, and she will one day be someone's mother and wife.

Your approach toward building a solid, God-honoring relationship should be like playing the game of baseball.

Hitting the ball in bounds is when you connect with her and establish that she is your girlfriend and/or someone you would like to continue getting to know better. Once you make the connection, it's time to move around the bases. Please be clear: The ultimate "score" isn't running game on her and disrespecting her or having sex with her. The ultimate score is that you develop a healthy relationship and that God is pleased with you and that you handle yourself in a God-honoring and responsible way during moments of temptation.

5 THOUGHTS ABOUT FIRST BASE

28. BE A GENTLEMAN

When you're on first base, you're getting to know her. It's vital that you are a gentleman and you handle yourself accordingly (whether in person, on the phone, in text messages, or any other setting). You want to always protect your witness and your integrity. The girl you're dating is someone's daughter, and she needs to be valued and respected. Regardless of whatever vibe she gives off, God is calling you to be a man of valor and to honor her in every way.

Also, when it comes to being a gentleman, it's not "old school" to open doors, pull out chairs when she's sitting down, or to allow her to order her food first when you're out on a date. Be patient with her. Let her know that you appreciate being in her space. When you set the tone in the beginning to be a gentleman, it makes everything else in the relationship flow. It's vital that you have a healthy relationship with God because when your relationship with God is on point, it will help you have the proper perspective on how to handle the girl you're dating.

29. TAKE IT SLOW

Build and establish the relationship. At this stage in your life, your focus is on getting to know other people and figure out your own likes and dislikes. Don't rush things in a dating relationship. Teenage dating should always be approached as a marathon and not a sprint. Take your time with her and your relationship. Don't be quick to fall for her or to allow her to fall for you. Remember, first base is the "getting to know you" stage. Pace yourself and make sure this is the right person to be with at the right time in your life. Taking it slow is important because far too often in the beginning, guys focus on impressing more than on being authentic. When you allow a period of time to pass, you will get to see the true person (and she will get to see the true you). Microwave relationships are never good! You can get it hot and heated really quickly, but it will get cold very fast!

30. DON'T BE A MISSIONARY

Don't act like you're married, and don't act like you're a missionary who dates non-Christian girls and tries to win them to Christ. Have balanced conversations where you're getting to know her both spiritually and intellectually. When it comes to dating, one of the biggest misconceptions as a Christian is that you can only have super spiritual conversation and cannot have any fun. That is far from the truth. Have fun and enjoy each other's company. Just make sure you're being intentional about what you do, what you say, and where you go. Don't be so heavenly minded that you're no earthly good. Keep the main thing the main thing. On first base, your objective is to get to know the true essence of who she is and to decide if you want to continue the relationship and to get to know her on a deeper level. Always keep your focus on the main goal.

31. DON'T JUDGE A BOOK BY ITS COVER

Just because she's a pretty girl who has a super hot body doesn't automatically mean she's the right one for you. Twice in 1 Corinthians, Paul said that everything is permissible, but not everything is beneficial (1 Corinthians 6:12 and 10:23). Make it a priority to always pray about who should be in your life. Looks are important because you want to be attracted to the person you're with, but paying attention to her heart will sustain the relationship. There are a lot of pretty girls with stink attitudes and wrong agendas.

Pray for discernment and wisdom when it comes to what type of girl you get into a relationship with. You have a responsibility and obligation to God and yourself to align yourself with like-minded people who will be more of an asset than a liability. Don't just pay attention to the outside. Make every effort to connect with her heart. What are her dreams, passions, thoughts, concerns, and worldview? Are you equally yoked, or is she just a hot chick and that's it? People judge the outside, but God judges the heart. Get to know her heart first, and everything else will follow.

32: "L" IS FOR "LEARN"

While on first base, always use the "L" word: LEARN! This is the time for learning who she is and not hooking up with her because of how fine she is. First base is the learning base. Don't have a lot of unrealistic expectations. Your job is to pray, listen, ask the right questions, and learn as much about her as you can. Knowledge is power, and God said in Hosea 4:6, *"My people are destroyed from lack of knowledge" (NIV)*. Do you know who you're dating—REALLY? If not, it may be a good idea to find out. It's always better to go into things with as much information as possible.

6 THOUGHTS ABOUT SECOND BASE

Now that you've gotten to know her and the relationship has progressed, it's time to establish some non-negotiable standards.

It's completely natural to feel more comfortable with a girl the more time you spend with her. But just because you're getting closer doesn't mean it's time to get "CLOSER." So while you're on second base, make the decision to maintain your character and integrity. Here are some thoughts to always keep in mind.

33. NEVER BE ALONE IN A HOUSE WITH HER

Don't put yourself in compromising situations. Being alone in the house with her is always dangerous because it puts you at risk of having your character and integrity challenged. Be wise about where you hang out together, and be committed to not putting yourself in a position that will ultimately make her or you uncomfortable. Plus, you don't want to be in a position where someone can accuse you of doing something that you didn't do.

34. KEEP THE BEDROOMS OFF LIMITS

This goes with the previous thought. It's too tempting, and you just can't trust yourself that much. Bedrooms are for sleeping—ALONE—until you're married and sharing a bed with your wife. If she wants to show you her room or you want to show her your room, take pictures and show it that way. Never be alone in the bedroom because it promotes an opportunity for sex and intimacy.

35. DON'T EXPECT YOUR RELATIONSHIP TO BE THE THING THAT FULFILLS YOU

That's putting too much pressure on yourself and the other person, and when the relationship ends, you're devastated because your life was built around that person and not God. Dating or a relationship is not designed to be the thing that validates you or fulfills you. God should always be the No. 1 person to validate and fulfill you. When you put other people in that role, you place them in the role of God—and that will never work.

36. ALWAYS KEEP THE ENDGAME IN MIND

You're dating this person, you're not married, and at the end of the day, you should just desire to have someone in your life whose company you enjoy and not someone you're looking to walk down the aisle with tomorrow. You are a teenager! When you become an adult, then you can do adult things. When you keep the end in mind, it's always a win-win situation. No one gets hurt because expectations and boundaries are established in the beginning.

37. BE AWARE OF YOUR PHYSICAL CONTACT

Know your triggers. If holding her hand gets you aroused, then keep your hands in your pocket. If you can't kiss her without wanting to have sex, then just shake her hand. Physical contact is the gateway to intimacy. Use great wisdom and discernment when it comes to how much is too much and what you should or shouldn't do. It's always best to move toward the side of caution and keep the physical contact to a minimum.

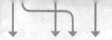

Even if she wants more, be the man God's calling you to be and lead in your relationship and say no.

38. DON'T PLAY WITH A GIRL'S EMOTIONS TO GET WHAT YOU WANT

That is called manipulation, and it's never cool. Always be open, upfront, and honest—even when it hurts. At the end of the day, she will appreciate it. Never lead a female on. Say what you mean and mean what you say. Date *one* female at a time. You're not a pimp, player, or hustler. That is not how God created you. Be a gentleman and respect her at all cost. Be the type of guy to her that you would want your sister or mom to have in her life. Don't be dishonest, and don't play games with her. It will always come back on you and will never end in your favor.

6 THOUGHTS ABOUT THIRD BASE

39. SEX IS NOT OVER AFTER THE MOMENT

A common misconception people have about sex is that once you do it, it's over with and you can move on to the next person. While that might make our conscience feel a little better, the reality is that it's not reality at all. Sex is as much emotional as it is physical. That means every time we have sex with someone, we are making an emotional and physical commitment. That's why sex was intended for couples that are married. Sex becomes a lifelong bond that you can't break without leaving a ton of scars. Even if you think you can avoid those scars, the reality is you can't.

40. STANDARDS ARE HARD TO ESTABLISH BUT EASY TO SACRIFICE

Parents and youth pastors do a great job in making the case for you to establish boundaries and standards that will help to sexually protect you. But to be honest, that's the easy part. The challenge comes long after the "True Love Waits" weekend or even after "the talk."

The challenge arrives when you're in the moment and every aspect of your body is telling you yes but the decision you made two weeks earlier to stay pure is saying no. It's that moment when your character and strength are tested that matters the most. That's when you'll decide if you want to be a man of God-honoring character.

41. MAKE SURE YOU'RE THINKING WITH YOUR HEAD

As a guy, you have one major thing working against you as it relates to sex: you. Yeah, we like to convince ourselves that this decision doesn't matter or that we can stop at any time. The reality is that the decision does matter and that we can't always stop ourselves. Sex and sexual urges aren't something that we can flip on and off like a switch and walk away. Think things through before you get into a situation or before you start to date that girl. Sex certainly has its consequences.

Getting a girl pregnant is only one consequence. Earlier we mentioned the emotional scars that can happen when you have sex before marriage, but don't forget that there are more than 25 STDs that exist that are bound to ruin your day.

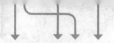

42. ONCE YOU CROSS PHYSICAL LINES, YOU CAN'T GO BACK

It can be a harsh and frustrating reality knowing that once you've crossed a line you can't "un-cross" it. With sex there aren't any "do-overs." This reality can be harsh because sometimes we just want to forget. We regret the decisions of the past and wish they never happened. It can also be frustrating because if you go too far with one girl, guess where you're gonna naturally try starting with the next? It becomes a bad cycle, and if you're not careful you'll throw in the towel, stop trying, and do whatever you want. And that's when everyone loses.

43. A LITTLE PASSION CAN LEAD TO A LIFETIME OF PAIN

A couple of years ago, a good friend of mine (Matty here) was over at the house, hanging out while watching football. We started to talk about high school and our "football days," being teenagers, and, of course, girls we dated. That's when the conversation turned.

He became pretty emotional as he talked about his high school love. They were inseparable, and most of us had known they had been sexually intimate. What I didn't know, until that night, is that he had gotten his girlfriend pregnant twice and she chose to have an abortion—both times. Shortly after high school they broke up and eventually married other people, but here he was, 20 years later, still dealing with the impact of bad decisions as a teenager. Our decisions might be "in the moment," but the impact lasts a lifetime.

44. MASTURBATION CANNOT BE A SUBSTITUTE FOR SEXUAL FULFILLMENT

Here is perhaps the most controversial subject of the entire book: *what to do with masturbation.* Some people will passionately advise you that masturbation is an act of lust and is wrong. Others will take the position that the physical release will keep you from crossing sexual lines with a girl and that it's permissible. Even in discussing this topic we debated the answer.

But here is what we stacked hands on:
Masturbation won't bring you fulfillment.

While masturbation might "scratch an itch," it is only addressing one aspect of fulfillment that God intended. That alone will leave you wanting more and will ignite a passion to search out what turns you on the most—and that's when you can really get burned.

CHAPTER 4

SPIRITUAL GROWTH & DISCIPLESHIP

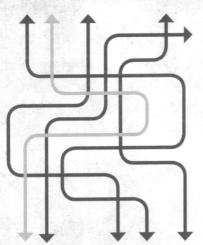

45. FINISH STRONG

Have you ever seen a race where someone slowed down at the end? When that happens, everyone knows that the runner did not do as well as they could have. Even if they win, they still didn't do their best. They left something out. They missed an opportunity to know that what they just gave was everything they had to give. It could have been better.

Not everything in life is a competition. But you probably take some pride in the things that you do. Everything you do reflects back on the type of person you are. You want to be seen as hard working, an honest man, and someone who can be trusted. That's why it's important to finish strong. When you finish strong, you show that you gave everything you could. Even when you are tired, get worn out, or lose interest, you want to finish with the best results possible because of what it says about you. Anytime you choose to start something, commit to finishing it strong. If you're going to do it, give it your best.

46. SEEK ACCOUNTABILITY IN YOUR LIFE

One of the greatest things about life is that we weren't made to be alone. We're created for relationships: parents, siblings, friends, even the church. Not only can those relationships help life to be more enjoyable, but they can also help you to be the best person you can be. You probably have goals and dreams for your life. Maybe it's to be a great husband, a reliable father, an effective leader, or a stronger Christian. Whatever your goals are, you don't have to go after them alone. Instead, it's important to have people in your life that will help you keep focused on your goals.

As iron sharpens iron, so a friend sharpens a friend (Proverbs 27:17). If you want to improve, to be sharper, to change bad behavior, or to be more focused, get people in your life that will help you to do so. Give them permission to ask you tough questions. Seek out someone who will speak honestly with you when you're making destructive choices, even when it's hard and it hurts—a person who will call you out on your junk and someone who has your best interests at heart, even when you don't. Want the best for your life? Find people who will help keep you on the right path.

47. TAKE YOUR GROWTH BY THE REINS

Ever had homework? Of course you have. You may not have done it, but you've definitely been given homework. Why do teachers do that? The answer is obvious: They want to punish you. Just kidding. Teachers give homework to help students learn the content. But there's another reason: to help students take some responsibility in their own educational growth. It would be easy if no one ever gave us homework. But without it, we'd run the risk of not really learning and growing the way that we could. We wish we could just learn it instantly, but that's not how things work.

If you want to grow, you have to take responsibility to help make that happen. Whether it's a hobby, a skill, a talent, or especially your faith in God, if you want to improve in an area and move forward, take the initiative. Other people—such as a teacher, a pastor, a parent, or a coach—can impact your growth. But they cannot *make* you do anything differently. All they can do is provide information, guidance, encouragement, and opportunity. It is up to you to decide what you will do about it. Step up to the challenge, own the responsibility, and take your growth by the reins.

48. KEEP A RIGHT PERSPECTIVE

Life isn't always easy, but you probably know that by now. Accidents happen, tragedy strikes, people are hurt, destruction hits, and things that we simply do not understand seem to interfere with life. In the middle of those experiences, it can be easy to get frustrated, become discouraged, or simply give up.

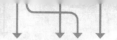

Here's what you might not know: That's what the enemy wants. God wants you to view life as a gift and as having purpose, and to trust God in the midst of all that happens. Satan wants to change that perspective, to get you to view God as some sort of mean, unloving bully in the sky. He'll use lies, confusion, and pain to turn your attention to the negative instead of the good and the hope that God offers. While God wants to spend life and eternity with you, Satan wants to separate you from God. It will come down to your choice, and that will include the perspective you choose for viewing the world. Choose hope with God.

49. STAY FOCUSED DURING FRUSTRATING TIMES

One of the most important things we have to do when trying to accomplish a goal is to stay focused. In the movie *Rocky IV*—the best one in the series, in my humble opinion (Mike here)—Rocky is in a battle with an incredibly strong opponent. Throughout the match, Rocky takes a beating. He gets knocked down again and again. Pretty frustrating, for sure.

But he keeps getting back up. Why? He knows what his goal is. He stays focused, even when things slow him down from success.

You will face situations in life that will frustrate you. You may not understand what is happening or why it's happening. All you will know is that it seems to be keeping you from accomplishing your goal. If you want to succeed, despite your circumstances, you have to stay focused. Give your frustrations to God; ask for wisdom and direction on how to handle the situation. Have a plan. Identify your goal, and go after it. You may have to deal with unexpected situations along the way, but don't lose sight of your target. You cannot succeed at anything if you do not know what the goal is. Stay focused.

50. PROTECT THE THINGS THAT ARE MOST IMPORTANT

We believe God has a plan for your life. We hope you believe that, too. We also know that your family likely has plans for your life. Your friends have plans for your life.

You have plans, hopes, dreams, and goals. But not everyone's plan for your life is right or good for you. Only you can choose which direction to go. That includes how you use your time, money, resources, talents, and other blessings in life. It is up to you to decide what is most important—not just what is the most fun, what's the easiest, or what will get you fame and fortune.

Remember this: What's right isn't always popular, and what's popular isn't always right. We have to determine what is most important to us. These are the essentials, the must-haves, the non-negotiables. Everything else may come and go, but for you to live your best life (which is the life God made you for), you will have to say no to some things. You may even have to say no to some really good things. But saying no to something means you can say yes to something better. Protect what's most important.

51. MAKE SCRIPTURE YOUR SOURCE OF WISDOM

The Bible is God's Word for us. Think about that for a moment. That's powerful. The Bible is a collection of stories, including parables and actual events, for us to learn from. Now ask yourself: Who are the people in your life you go to for advice? More than likely, you seek those people because of their experiences, wisdom, and what you think they know. God—the creator of the universe, the maker of you, the all-knowing and all-powerful one—has given us words to learn from. All through Scripture we find examples of success stories and failures, stories of mistakes and how God can use everything for good. God shares his love for us, and he helps us see that we are created for a purpose and that we can live with hope.

The Bible exists to help us understand truth and, ultimately, the best way to live. If you had a choice between "good enough" and "best," you'd want "best" every time, right? Scripture is a vital resource as we seek out and understand the wisest decisions we can make.

Wise does not mean easy, because sometimes we will be in situations that aren't easy. But when everything is said and done, following wisdom is the best choice we can make. If you're serious about wanting what's best in your life, go to Scripture. There's no greater source of wisdom in the world.

52. PRAYER IS YOUR LIFELINE

We all need connection in life—sources of input, refreshment, energy, feedback, and relationship. It can come through people, books, trips, hobbies, games, and all kinds of other various forms. As great as all of those things are, they cannot be with you everywhere you go. What if there was a way, regardless of where you went and what you did, to have a direct connection with God? That's where prayer comes in. As soon as you read the word *prayer*, something came to mind, didn't it? Let's keep it simple, though: Prayer is simply talking to God. It doesn't require fancy words or long sentences. It's just you and God communicating.

No matter what situation you are in, you have a direct line to the Creator of the universe. That's awesome. God is with you and wants to be with you all the time—not just to see what you do, but also to share in your experiences with you. In any relationship, communication is huge. The same goes for your relationship with God. Share your hurts and needs. Share your good news and excitement. Ask for guidance and wisdom. People may let you down, but God will always be with you. Make God your go-to conversation every time.

53. PRACTICE MAKES PERFECT

If you want to improve at something in life, you have to actually be doing that something. To improve your basketball skills, spend time dribbling, shooting, blocking, and handling. If you want to grow as a guitarist, you practice playing the guitar. If you want to get stronger, you lift weights. You don't just think about doing something; you do it—over and over.

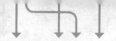

The same thing goes for our spiritual growth and disciplines. If you want to improve your prayer time with God, spend time praying. Want to develop stronger relationships with Christ-followers? Spend time with some. How about reading the Bible? Take time each day and read. Remember, no one is an all-star at anything on day one. Things may come more naturally to some people, but practice is still necessary to grow and improve. Start with small steps and work your way forward. Be consistent in your commitment—that will give you the best opportunity to grow.

54. AS YOUR ROUTINE CHANGES, YOU HAVE TO BE INTENTIONAL

We know from experience that life never stays the same. Change happens. We move to a new home. We start a new hobby. Our class schedule gets mixed up. Work hours are revised. Things can throw a curveball into our daily routines. When that happens, it can be an easy excuse to *not* do something.

What you do with your time communicates what is important to you. If one of your goals is to spend time daily with God, designate time in your schedule to do so. Whenever your routine changes, it can be easy to let your devotional time or Bible-reading time go on the back burner. "I'll do it tomorrow," you say. Then the next day. Then the next. Pretty soon you're in a new routine. Your intentions may be good, but they don't matter if nothing happens. Be intentional with your time. When your schedule changes, prioritize things so that you don't drop what you know you need to get done.

55. FORGIVENESS IS KEY TO MOVING FORWARD

Life can be difficult sometimes. Bad things happen. Situations get out of our control. Some of the most painful experiences in life can be the result of what someone else has done (or hasn't done) and how it impacts us. In those moments we can develop a bitter, unforgiving attitude toward those people. In the eyes of the world, that might make sense.

Some people believe that if someone has done you wrong, don't let them forget it. They owe you. Get revenge. Hold a grudge.

The danger is that living this way will keep you locked in an emotional prison. Holding on to pain, hurt feelings, and anger will not help you to move past the situation. Revenge won't change what happened. Any time you think about it, you'll be sucked right back in. You won't be past it. It will have a hold on you.

In order to move forward, do what may be the hardest thing to do: forgive. Release them from their wrong. This may seem like a weak approach or a coward's way, but it takes strength to forgive. It's easy to hold a grudge. It's not easy to forgive. A grudge will keep you stuck somewhere. Forgiveness lets you move forward. When you forgive someone, that person may not accept it or even care, but it allows you to let go.

Something else to consider: If we're honest, we've all messed up. We've all made mistakes. We've all sinned against God.

God loves us—so much so that he gave his Son, Jesus, as a sacrifice so that we could be forgiven. If God would forgive us for all that we've done wrong, shouldn't we be willing to forgive others as well?

Easy? No. The best way to live? Absolutely.

56. WORDS ARE NO MATCH FOR ACTIONS

Ever meet someone who says one thing but does another? Maybe you're even guilty of being that guy sometimes. If someone says "this" but does "that," what do you think is really the truth for him? If I (Mike) told you how honest of a guy I am, but you see me cheating on homework all the time, you're going to know that what I've said isn't true. It's very easy to say the right things. But we know that what people *do* is usually more important than the things people *say*.

If I want to know what you really believe, I would watch the way you live, not just listen to the things you tell me.

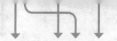

The phrase "actions speak louder than words" is true for all of us. Words can be empty, but the way you live speaks volumes. People believe something about you by the way you live. What have you been telling them?

57. ACTIONS ARE THE RESULT OF A CHANGED HEART

There are times when we know that something needs to change in our life. We need to be men of integrity. We need to be kind to people. We need to be careful about the words we use. Whatever it is, simply knowing what needs to happen won't actually change anything. A chain smoker may know he needs to stop smoking, but knowledge alone doesn't change anything. An athlete who wants to improve his skills knows it will take practice, but that doesn't change anything—not on its own, at least. Knowledge or awareness is only part of the solution. For change to happen, you must take something from head knowledge and move it to your heart.

Here's what we mean: You can know what needs to happen, but if you don't move beyond that, it won't matter. You have to take it to heart and live it out. When you move something from head to heart, it will come out in your actions. If there's an area in your life that needs to change, don't ignore it. Identify it. Ask God to work change in your heart. Pray for strength and wisdom. Make a plan. Then move forward. Don't settle for knowledge. Strive for a changed heart.

58. WHAT'S IN YOUR HEART COMES OUT IN YOUR ACTIONS

A person can look at the way you live and tell what you believe. Not what you say you believe, but what you *actually* believe in your heart. We're not talking about your physical heart that pumps blood. We mean that deep part of your mind, your conscience that determines your values, priorities, and how you live. What you believe comes out in the way that you live. This is not "believe" in the sense of knowledge of the right answer, but what you think is the most beneficial way for you to live.

If I (Mike) believe that being a great friend is important, I won't talk behind someone's back. If I believe it's more important for me to fit in, I'll talk about anyone, anywhere, anytime in order to get there. Even when we know in our head what's right, it's what in our heart that comes out in the way we live. You may like everything about the way that you live. But if you see something in you that needs to change and improve, that's good. That's part of maturing. Pay attention to the way that you live, and you'll see what you believe.

CHAPTER 5

LEADERSHIP

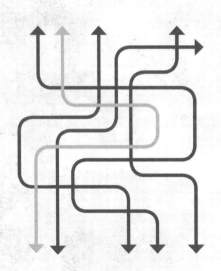

59. AS MEN, GOD HAS CALLED US TO THE RESPONSIBILITY OF LEADERSHIP

If you are a man, congratulations! You've been chosen to carry the responsibility of leadership. That doesn't mean women are not called to leadership, but as men, we have a unique calling to be leaders. You cannot take this lightly. For example, consider if you hope to be married and have children. We are called to be leaders in our household. The decisions we make and the ways we choose to go will directly influence our family. It will affect your wife and your relationship with her. Your children will look to you as an example of what a God-honoring man and father should be. That may seem like a lot of weight to carry, but leadership is an incredible opportunity—one that God has given us because we have the potential to thrive at it. In whatever ways you lead, lead with integrity, honesty, and focus.

60. GOD USES THE ORDINARY TO LEAD GREATLY

Throughout the Bible, we find examples of how God used ordinary men to lead through extraordinary situations. God did not wait for people to reach a certain level of achievement. God did not choose to use people simply because they were in positions of authority. Instead, God went with those who chose to follow him.

Sometimes these guys were not even particularly skilled or trained in the way God used them. God chose David, a shepherd boy who watched sheep for a living, to kill a giant and later to become the king of Israel. He used Moses, a guy with a speech problem, to speak on God's behalf and to lead millions of people out of slavery— using a path opened directly through the Red Sea! God used ordinary, average fishermen and labor workers to begin the church—not scholars or professors! Seriously, guys who fished for a living helped launch a world-changing movement involving billions of people who have chosen to follow Jesus.

That's incredible! Something else that's incredible: God wants to use you to do great things, too!

61. LEADERSHIP IS INFLUENCE-DRIVEN

One of the simplest ways to understand leadership is to think about influence. A leader influences people toward a decision. Think about any leader. Whoever came to mind, that person influenced people to follow a certain path. A coach influences his team to play a certain way. A parent can influence a child's behavior.

Not all leaders are good. Some leaders have influenced followers to make terrible choices. But they were leaders because of their influence.

You have the ability to influence the lives of people around you: family, friends, classmates, co-workers, teammates. That's actually a powerful opportunity for you.

You have the ability to influence people for good or for bad by the things you say, do, don't say, and don't do. Sounds a little heavy, huh? What it means is that you should not take your leadership or influence lightly. You have the ability to try to lead people toward greater things. If your friends are looking to make destructive choices, you have the ability to guide them a different direction. Stand your ground when you know you need to. In those moments, people will see what you stand for—and that could influence a person more than you know.

62. LEADERSHIP ISN'T A POWER TRIP

One of the dangerous things about being in leadership is letting it go to your head. Being a leader isn't about your own personal gain. Leadership is about doing what is best for the greater good. It's not about being the boss and getting everything the way you want it. In leadership, there can be rewards, success, and a sense of being important. Those are not bad things. The trouble comes when you use your position to get things for yourself.

Maybe it's respect. Maybe it's something of value. But leadership isn't about you.

The greatest leaders know what needs to happen and why it needs to happen. It's not for themselves; it's for those who are in need. George Washington was a leader because people deserved freedom. Martin Luther King Jr. was a leader because people deserved equal rights. Do those things benefit the leader? Yes, sometimes they do. Were those leaders willing to sacrifice for the cause? Absolutely, because the cause, the goal is what their leadership was about. Leadership isn't about power; it's about accomplishing what needs to be done.

63. GREAT LEADERS ARE CALLED TO BE HUMBLE

It can be a great feeling to have people following you. When leaders accomplish goals, they can swell up with pride. It's easy to get swept up in the moments and feelings. When that happens, even in a small way, people sometimes mistakenly make the feelings and successes about themselves.

They think of how great they are and point to the big ways that they have led people.

Here is the question we must ask: How did they get there? The reality is that no leader got to where they are on their own. They had help. Ultimately, they are in positions of leadership because God allowed them to be. In fact, God may have specifically called them to be there. With any leader, despite all of their power and authority, God could end it all in an instant. Leadership is a gift and a responsibility. It's not about you. Stay humble and grateful that God would allow you to have the opportunity.

64. LEADERS DON'T SUPPRESS SOMEONE ELSE

In leadership, we know what our goal is. When our heart is focused on the cause instead of our own selfish motives, we are able to lead better. Focusing on ourselves limits our ability to lead. Leadership should not be about us, but about the goal.

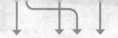

Think about this situation. You have two basketball teams, each with a team captain. Captain A likes to be the star of the game, while Captain B will do what he can to get the ball to other players—even players better than he is—in order to help the team win. Captain A makes sure he gets as much playing time as possible, while Captain B is willing to sit so he can put the best players on the court for the situation. Which captain was the better leader? Captain B. He was less concerned about maintaining his status and more concerned with success as a team.

When you stop others from opportunities to shine, you greatly limit what you will ever be able to accomplish. Focus more on the goal and less on yourself. When that happens, the chance for success increases in big ways.

65. TAKE RESPONSIBILITY FOR YOUR IMPACT

Take a moment and think of any famous person. Now think about what difference that person has made in the world, big or small. Now think of another person, someone you know. Think about what difference this individual has made. What's interesting is that every person you know—or know of—has made an impact. That means you will also make an impact. Regardless of the size of your impact, it will happen.

It's important to remember that whatever we do, we are responsible for it. Whatever impact you make in the life of one person, your friends, your family, your team, the world—take responsibility for it. You cannot determine what people will think or say about you, but you can be intentional about making the best impact possible, wherever you are. Now you have the opportunity to make sure your impact is worth making.

66. LEADERS COME ALONGSIDE OTHERS

In leadership, we have the opportunity to recognize situations that aren't what they should or could be. Sometimes these are things that we can begin to tackle directly. Other times, there are people who are already addressing the situation, and the best thing we can do is jump in. It's a way of saying, "Hey, this is important, and we need to help take care of it."

Leadership in this regard means stepping in to add additional help, support, and strength to a cause. Think of it like this: Picture an auto accident with two vehicles, and both have passengers and both cars are on fire. The police department doesn't sit back and watch because the fire company arrived first. They're jumping in to help, because what's at stake is important. Leaders take initiative to come alongside others whenever and however they can.

67. YOU'RE NEVER TOO YOUNG TO LEAD

One of the greatest truths about leadership is that it is not limited by your age. Regardless of how old or young you are, you are capable of leading. That doesn't mean it is easy, especially for those who may be older than you. This situation is actually talked about in the Bible. Paul, an older man, offered words of encouragement to Timothy, who was a young guy. Paul wrote these words: *Don't let anyone think less of you because you are young. Be an example to all believers in what you say, in the way you live, in your love, your faith, and your purity (1 Timothy 4:12).* Essentially Paul is saying that age doesn't matter. You have the opportunity to show people the best way to do things. As people see what you are doing, they may be influenced to change and follow your example. Your friends, even your youngest friends, are following someone's influence. Be a good example.

68. LEADERS DON'T SHIRK THEIR RESPONSIBILITY

Being in a position of leadership is a gift and a responsibility. It's something that we should not take lightly, because it will make a difference in people's lives and situations. There are times when we may step out of a position of leadership, during certain seasons of life. But anytime you are in a role of leadership, you are responsible to do what you are there to do—even when it's hard.

Imagine a coach deciding he doesn't want to tell the team what play to run, doesn't want to sub people in and out when needed, or doesn't even want to show up at the game. That coach isn't being responsible for what he's there to do. And that's not leadership. True leaders fulfill their responsibilities the best way they can, regardless of the situation. Step up and own it.

69. LEADERSHIP IS NOT VOID OF CONFLICT

Imagine never having a tough situation or disagreement with anyone in your life. As nice as that would be, we know that's not how it is. But have you ever considered that might not be a bad thing? Conflict means that there's more than one opinion about something. It also doesn't always mean that someone is wrong.

In leadership, you know what you want to accomplish. As you work to move in that direction, you will encounter people along the way who may see other ways of accomplishing the goal. Instead of avoiding conflict, engage in the conversation. Make sure that you keep everyone's eyes focused on the goal. Process through the options and outcomes. Then move forward with the best choice. Sometimes that may not be the approach you originally wanted, but that's OK because our goal is to move forward, not to always have things our way. Understand that conflict is a natural part of being in leadership. If you never face resistance, you may not be moving very far.

70. SOMETIMES LEADERSHIP MEANS BEING A FOLLOWER

Sometimes in life, one person has an idea or does something that seems a little too crazy or different for people. It may be a great thing, but it means people would have to stop doing what is comfortable and familiar. Each person has the ability to look at that idea or something on their own and evaluate whether or not it is a good thing, but many times people simply follow where everyone else is going. Great opportunities can be missed this way.

Instead of going with the crowd, sometimes leadership means that we become the first follower of the vision someone else shares. Imagine a room with a line drawn down the middle; one person with a great idea is on the left, and everyone else is on the right. A leader has the opportunity to cross that line to the other side. It may not be their idea, but they see the potential. When that happens, they have the opportunity to influence people to take the risk and come along. Sometimes leading means following.

CHAPTER 6

IDENTITY

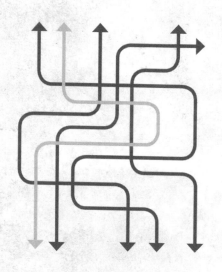

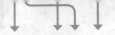

3 THOUGHTS ON HOW YOUR LIFE IS INTENTIONAL

71. GOD KNEW YOU BEFORE YOU WERE BORN

Jeremiah 1:5 says, *"Before I formed you in the womb I knew you, before you were born, I set you apart; I appointed you prophet to the nations" (NIV).*

So what does that mean to you? It means that your life has meaning, purpose, and value. God was intentional when he allowed you to be conceived by your parents. You are not a tragedy or a mistake—even if your parents aren't together or don't get along, or you're adopted, or you don't know your parents at all. God knew you before you were born, and now that you're here, it's time for you to eliminate excuses and begin living your life with purpose. You're here for a reason! You matter to God.

72. GOD CALLED YOU TO DO SOMETHING

Jeremiah 29:11 says, *"For I know the plans I have for you,"* declares the Lord, *"plans to prosper you and not to harm you, plans to give you hope and a future" (NIV).*

God has called you to do something beyond what you can think or imagine. He has a plan for you, and his plan is greater than any plan that you could ever have for yourself. You're called to do something and not to just exist. You're more than a male, son, brother, or student. You're God's gift to the world, and you have something specific and unique to do. In the midst of all of the good, bad, ups, and downs, God has a plan for you, and you're here by design.

73. GOD HAS CALLED YOU TO BE GODLY

*But **you** are a chosen people, a royal priesthood, a holy nation, God's special possession (1 Peter 2:9 NIV, emphasis added).*

You are built for greatness. No one can beat *you* at being *you*! If they try, they will only be a cheap copy of a great original. Your identity is found in God. He and he alone has a plan for you that will always work and will never fail. God is calling you to live your life from the inside out and to honor God in all that you do and say. Walk the way God wants you to walk, and live the way God wants you to live. With him, you never lose; with him, you always win!

6 THOUGHTS ON HOW GOD DEFINES YOUR LIFE

74. YOUR FAMILY LIFE DOESN'T DEFINE YOU

Believe it or not, you are not defined by your family and friends. Their flaws, mistakes, mishaps, and sins don't make or break you. (The latest fashions, styles, and trends don't define you, either.) You are defined by the plan God has for you. You're not "just like that one."

You're not going to end up "just like they did."
Follow Christ and allow him to lead and direct
your path.

75. GOD HAS A PLAN FOR YOUR LIFE

You are created in the image of God, so that
means you are an amazing individual all by
yourself! God's plan will always be better than
anything anyone else can come up with for you.
God knows what's best for you and what you
need. God created you for a time such as now,
and your life (with its good and bad moments)
has meaning. Turn your trials into testimonies,
and move from being the victim to seeing
yourself as victorious. You are special to God,
and no matter what others say, you have value to
the kingdom of God!

76. LIVE FOR AN AUDIENCE OF ONE

Your desire should be to live to please an
audience of one (your Heavenly Father)
not many.

God's plan for you outweighs any other plans you may have for your life. Always make sure your self-image is God's image of you and not the image the world says you should have. When you live to please an audience of one, it doesn't matter when the haters hate on you because you realize their voice has no power or merit. What do you hear God saying to you about who you are?

77. DON'T CONFORM TO THE WORLD

The world is always changing and evolving, but God is consistent and never changes. He is the same yesterday, today, and forever more. Be authentic and true to yourself. Our culture says that what's in today will be out tomorrow, and what's hot this morning will be insignificant this afternoon. But Romans 12:2 offers this wisdom: *Don't conform to the patterns of this world, but be transformed by the renewing of your mind (NIV).* This means getting your mind in a place where it's focused on the things of God and not the things of the world. Get your mind right and get in the game!

78. SHOWING EMOTION IS OK

As men we're taught to be tough and not to show our feelings, but when you're secure in who you are, you're OK with expressing yourself to others. When Jesus died on the cross, he showed a wide range of emotion. He showed compassion for the thief and others, as well as pain and sorrow. Being a *real* man isn't about being tough and rough; it's about being authentic and genuine. Being a *real* man is being true to yourself and your emotions. Don't shy away from showing emotions. When you're in a place of freedom and vulnerability, that's when God can use you the most.

79. MAKE SURE YOUR SELF-IMAGE IS GOD'S IMAGE OF YOU

How do you see yourself—REALLY? Do you see yourself the way God sees you? If not, why not? In Genesis 1:27, God said that we are created in his own image.

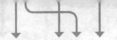

That means when you were created, not only were you on the mind of God, but you were in the plans of God. Because you are God's creation, you look like him. And if you are part of God's family, you can become more like him. Does that mean you have to be perfect every day? Absolutely not! As followers of Christ, our desire should be to daily strive to be Christ-like. Some days will be better than others, and that's OK. When you begin to see yourself the way God sees you, you will walk, talk, act, and live differently. Instead of living on accident, you will begin to live on purpose.

CHAPTER 7

LEGACY

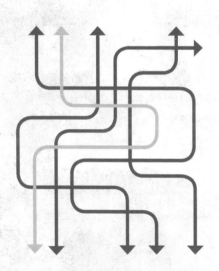

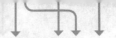

80. GET OUT OF YOUR COMFORT ZONE

Making any sort of impact, whether today or tomorrow, requires doing some things that force us to get out of our comfort zone. Life isn't meant to be lived within a bubble. Rather, we are called to take a calculated risk that will result in making an impact on those around us.

When Jesus called 12 men to follow him as his closest disciples, he was asking them to leave the lives they knew and the jobs they had, and to accept a higher calling for their lives. It wasn't easy, but it was simple. Hard choices would lie ahead of them, but everything boiled down to what Jesus was calling them to do. So, what is he stirring inside of you?

81. FIND SOMEONE TO IMPACT AND INFLUENCE

Your life has to have intentionality behind it. Taking on a challenge for no other reason than just to take it on will lead to boredom and pride.

But if you ask, "Whose life can I impact today?" then you're figuring out what life is really about!

One gentleman that I (Matty) think of as my mentor lives with the intention of figuring out how to make the lives of people he comes in contact with better. This doesn't always mean he says something nice, but the intent is always there: *I don't want to miss this opportunity.* Everyone's life is unique and significant. Who in your life would benefit from your investment in them today?

82. STRIVE FOR A "ONE-SENTENCE" LIFE

Who has had the biggest impact on your life? A parent? A teacher? A coach? What has made their impact so significant in who you are today? How would you describe their life? Chances are good that this individual wouldn't want you to write a report about their life, but they probably would say something like, "When my life is over, all I want people to say about me is...."

At the end of the day, when your life is all through, there will be one sentence on your tombstone—one thing you'll be known for. Today is when you write that story. Today is when you determine what people will say about you when your time on earth is done.

83. LIFE IS AS MUCH ABOUT WHO YOU ARE AS WHAT YOU DO

While it's really important to "do," it's more important to "be." We can never lose sight of the fact that who we are on the inside greatly impacts what we do on the outside. If our character isn't right, then our attitude will reveal that and will corrupt our impact. Life isn't as much about what you do as it is the mindset you have in the process.

84. YOUR REPUTATION DOES MATTER

People may try to make you look bad, and they may do it at times when you least expect it.

Maybe it's because your personalities don't mesh, they don't like the color of your skin or where you grew up, or they hate the fact that you stand up for your beliefs. Regardless of their reasons, you can expect that some people may stab you in the back and lie about you. And while you can't control what they say or do, you do have a huge weapon to your advantage: your reputation.

Your reputation will stand against the lies and character attacks. If you're consistent in who you are and how you respond, people won't have a reason to question your character or reputation. But if you've given them reasons to doubt you, then you're in trouble. And there is little recovery when people start to question your character. Protect it at all costs, even if you must sacrifice popularity, money, and advancement.

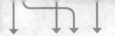

85. LEGACY MEANS LIVING FOR TOMORROW

If we're not careful, we will live our lives for today with no thought of tomorrow. The Bible warns us not to be overly concerned about tomorrow because we don't know what the days will bring. Jesus was very careful to remind us not to become consumed with the everyday tasks of life and to balance it with a bigger picture on life, including the eternal impact our lives can have.

Paul reminded us in Philippians 3 that the accomplishments he had in his life could in no way compare with the reward that he would one day receive in heaven. He reminded us that he pressed forward toward this prize. We can never ignore the impact our legacy may have on those around us and those who will follow us. For some it might mean they choose to begin following Christ, and others may be influenced to try a little harder and live a little more purely. Our job is to pass our faith on to the next person in line.

86. TAKE A SNAPSHOT, AND MAKE ADJUSTMENTS

I (Matty) love technology, but I hate to take care of it. I've dropped my phone so many times that it doesn't even look like an iPhone® anymore. The front screen is shattered, the back looks even worse, and the case that's supposed to save it is taped together! But the greatest amount of damage is on the inside. The hardware is shot, the phone fritzes out, and the camera is off. Taking any sort of picture is a waste of time.

A picture helps me capture the moment and reflect on what's there. Without the picture, that moment in time is lost. Taking a "snapshot" of our life helps us to take inventory of what's there and see any adjustments that we need to make. Making time to pause, reflect, and take inventory helps to ensure that we're headed in the right direction.

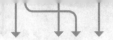

87. PERCEPTION IS REALITY

The challenging part of leadership and legacy is we have to be honest with ourselves and let other people be honest with us as well. We might think we are having one level of impact on their lives, but the reality could be something totally different. While we might be having a real impact in our world, the possibility exists that we can also have huge holes in our leadership. Allowing people to share what they perceive about our leadership opens up their hearts to us and gives us a genuine opportunity for life-change. Openness assumes vulnerability and trust. And people have to know that they can trust us with how we're living our lives.

88. WHAT LEGACY HAS IMPACTED YOU?

Every legacy has a beginning, that beautiful moment in time when one life reaches out in humility to touch another. It is in that moment, and the many that follow, when a spark is ignited and a passion for excellence is unearthed.

Every life has been touched by another person who had a certain of undeniable significance.

At times, that spark is hidden beneath a layer of fear, doubt, or frustration. But give it time, and the persistent fanning of that spark will overcome those emotions. As you look into your heart and life, who is that person for you? Was it a coach, a parent, a teacher, or a friend? We all have someone who believes in us. Who is lighting the path for you?

89. MAKE IT EASIER FOR THE NEXT GENERATION

The goal of a legacy is to pave the way for the next generation to come. Psalm 78 paints a beautiful portrait of what it means to remind people not only of where they came from but also where they're headed. Without reminders of past struggles and victories, we can never appreciate our future. Likewise, without knowing where we're headed, we can never honor our past. The two are eternally connected, woven within our DNA.

Selfishly, we can look at the next generation as a hindrance and inconvenience. Maturely, we can view them as a hammer and chisel ready to carve out the next formation of our culture. Remarkably, we play a part in seeing the masterpiece completed.

90. COURAGE CAN COST YOU

Having the courage to lead and make a difference in someone's life is never an easy decision. We commonly mistake courage as the absence of fear, but courage actually is *revealed in* moments of fear or apprehension. The reality is that courage is only present when there's fear.

Courage recognizes that the decisions we make might cost us a friendship, a job, or even our life—but we continue to push forward. What decisions have you been too afraid to move forward with? What isn't being accomplished in your life because of fear? Don't let the fear paralyze you, but rather use the opportunity to, as the Bible says, "be of good courage."

CHAPTER 8

ACCEPTANCE

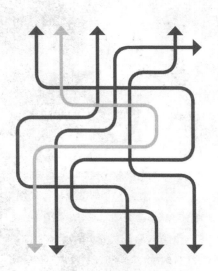

3 THOUGHTS ON SOCIAL INJUSTICE

91. STAND UP FOR THOSE WHO ARE OPPRESSED

Growing up, my (Matty here) view of the world was very limited. We didn't have the Internet, Skype®, or Facebook®. "My world" consisted of my neighborhood, the few cities that were close by, and the state of Kentucky. Needless to say, my perspective had certain limitations.

But with today's technology, we're all connected with the world in ways I could have never imagined. The world has become our "neighborhood," and we're exposed not just to "cool" parts of another country but to their hurt as well. We can see the oppressed, the hungry, and the desperate—in our own communities, in our nation, and around the world.

As we look from our "window," we can choose to turn away or to speak for those without a voice and fight for those without the strength.

92. GET INVOLVED IN THE SOLUTION

I (Matty) hate getting my hands dirty, and I love writing checks. When I see a video at church concerning digging a well in Kenya, helping out schools in Detroit, or serving the elderly in India, I typically feel bad and eagerly give money to the cause. And while that's good, I don't think that's the response Jesus is really wanting.

In Matthew 25, he tells of how one day, some people will be told to get away from him because they weren't moved with compassion enough to put their faith in action and "inconvenience" themselves. To follow Christ means getting in the game, getting our hands dirty, and doing some things we normally wouldn't do. We have to put people first.

93. IF YOU'RE NOT MOVED BY SUFFERING, YOU'VE NOT CONNECTED WITH THE HEART OF CHRIST

Christ came to the earth because he was moved with compassion. Humanity had sinned, and the only way for us to have forgiveness of sins and restoration of our relationship with God was for Jesus to lay down his life. While that was the greatest example of compassion, he also cared just as deeply for the everyday needs of people. To ignore the needs of people is to ignore the mission and heart of Christ. Jesus calls us to a life of sacrifice, service, and significance, and that is what changes the world.

4 THOUGHTS ON PREJUDICE

94. DON'T LET PEOPLE HOLD YOU TO THEIR STEREOTYPES

Unfortunately, in life some people are going to stereotype you based on how they see you or perceive you. The prejudice in the world isn't always a white, Asian, Hispanic, or black thing. As you live, learn, and discover who you are, recognize that people are going to label you, but you don't have to accept their label. Remember, it's not what people call you; it's what you answer to.

Also, it's vital that you don't judge a book by its cover. Don't be a hater! Just as you shouldn't allow people to hold you to their stereotype, don't stereotype people either.

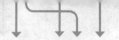

95. REMEMBER THAT THEIR DIFFERENCES DON'T MAKE THEM BAD

Just because you meet people who may look, talk, act, or even believe differently than you doesn't mean they're bad; it just means they're different. We live in a big world with a wide variety of views and perspectives. Don't try to force your beliefs on anyone; if someone's beliefs need changing, let God do it. What makes relationships special is when we are in a position to learn from one another. Differences can help broaden our horizon and give us more compassion for people who are not like us. Be open to learning new things and loving people for who they are, not for what they stand for.

96. NATIONALISM IS NOT THE SAME AS PATRIOTISM

We're Christians first, and Christ died for everyone, not just the people in our own nation. We're one nation under God—but God also loves every other nation!

So as you strive daily to be Christ-like, strive to love those who Christ loved, regardless of where they come from or where they live. You can be patriotic; just don't be prejudiced. Respect everyone and treat people the way you want to be treated. Respect isn't always earned; sometimes it's just given. Give people the respect you would want them to give you.

97. WE'RE CHRIST-FOLLOWERS FIRST

Regardless of our different views, ideas, perspective, and thoughts, we're called to be Christ-followers first. As followers of Jesus, God commands us in Matthew 22:36-40 to first love him with all of our heart and with all of our soul and with our entire mind—then he commands us to love our neighbor as we love ourselves. As followers of Christ, we are called to love everyone, no matter what. When it comes to learning about acceptance, love is the great equalizer!

2 THOUGHTS ON RACISM

98. RACISM LOOKS DIFFERENT TODAY BUT STILL EXISTS

Racism is a very hard thing to talk about and address. Sadly, even in today's culture, racism is still very much a part of our world. We cannot be fooled and think racism no longer exists, and as Christ-followers, we need to be committed to be a part of the situation and not the problem. Never judge or disassociate yourself from someone because of the color of their skin or because they may have been born in a different part of town from you.

When Paul wrote *Do not be yoked together with unbelievers* in 2 Corinthians 6:14 (NIV), he wasn't saying, "Don't talk to people who have a different race or socio-economic background." He was talking about spiritual differences. Race and ethnicity and skin color don't have to divide us.

99. LOOK AT PEOPLE'S CHARACTER AND NOT THEIR COLOR

There are no longer whites-only and blacks-only restaurants, bathrooms, water fountains, and schools. However, there are many places and people that still experience the same type of racism and injustices as they did in the 1960s during the Civil Rights movement. As a Christ-follower, you are called to love everyone equally and not to hate or discriminate against anyone.

God is a God of love, hope, and equality. Dr. Martin Luther King Jr. said this during his "A Testament of Hope" speech: "Darkness cannot drive out darkness: only light can do that. Hate cannot drive out hate: only love can do that." When you look at people, don't look at the color of their skin; look at the character that lies within them.